MW01278515

Desert Animals

By Christy Steele

Raintree Steck-Vaughn Publishers

A Harcourt Company

Austin · New York

www.raintreesteckvaughn.com

Published by Raintree Steck-Vaughn Publishers, an imprint of Steck-Vaughn Company.

Library of Congress Cataloging-in-Publication Data
Steele, Christy.
   Desert animals / Christy Steele.
      p. cm. -- (Animals of the biomes)
   Summary: Discusses the physical characteristics, behavior, and habitat of various animals that live in the desert biome.
   Includes bibliographical references (p.).
   Contents: Animals in the desert -- The roadrunner -- The giant desert hairy scorpion -- The camel -- The gila monster -- What will happen to desert animals? -- Quick facts
   ISBN 0-7398-5686-3 (hc); 0-7398-6406-8 (pbk).
    1. Desert animals--Juvenile literature. [1. Desert animals. 2. Desert ecology. 3. Ecology.] I. Title. II Series.

QL116 .S74 2002
591.754--dc21   2002067911

Printed and bound in the United States of America.
1 2 3 4 5 6 7 8 9 10 WZ 05 04 03 02 01

Produced by Compass Books

Photo Acknowledgments
Glenn M. Oliver, cover; R. Arndt, 1, 27; Joe McDonald, 8, 16, 39, 42, 44, 45; W. Anderson, 11; Anthony Merieca, 13, 14, 20; Doug Sokell, 18, 44; Bob Newman, 30; Jim Merli, 32, 35, 36; Jack Michanowski, 40; Inga Spence, 24; Image 100, 45.

Content Consultant
Dr. Steve Munzinger
Biology Dept., Briar Cliff University
Sioux City, IA

This book supports the National Science Standards.

Contents

Many animals in hot deserts like this one live inside cracks in rocks.

Animals in the Desert

Many people think that deserts are lifeless places full of sand, but they are much more than that. The desert is an interesting **biome** full of living things. A biome is a large region, or area, made of communities. A community is a group of certain plants and animals that live in the same place.

There are two kinds of deserts, hot deserts and cold deserts. Cold deserts have long cold seasons and short warm seasons. Hot deserts are warm all year round. All deserts receive less than 10 inches (25 cm) of rain or snow each year. The temperatures in the desert change greatly from day to night. It can be very hot during the day and very cold at night.

Arctic Ocean

North America

Europe

Asia

Atlantic Ocean

Pacific Ocean

Africa

South America

Indian Ocean

Australia

N
W E
S

Deserts
Oceans
Continents

Antarctica

Deserts cover about one-seventh of Earth. This map shows where the major deserts are.

What Lives in the Deserts?

Animal and plant species that are found in deserts have adapted to survive in the desert's extreme conditions. To adapt means that a species changes over time to fit well where it lives.

Certain kinds of plants have adapted to live in the desert. Deserts can have many different kinds of soil. Some deserts are sandy, while other deserts are covered by gravel, fine clay, or rocky soil. Various kinds of plants grow in the soil of each desert. There are few trees in deserts. Many plants are short because shorter plants need less water to grow. Most desert plants have long roots that reach deep into the soil to find water.

Desert animals must be able to live in very hot or very cold temperatures. To do this, some animals in the hot desert are active only at night when it is cooler. During the day, they hide under rocks or in **burrows** to keep cool. A burrow is a hole or tunnel made by an animal to live in.

Most desert animals are small. It is hard for large animals to find shade from the sun. They also need less water to live. All animals must find ways to **conserve** water. To conserve means to save. Many desert animals have ways to conserve water and store food inside their bodies.

This book tells about four different kinds of desert animals—roadrunners, giant desert hairy scorpions, camels, and gila monsters. In the following chapters, you will find out how each of these animals has adapted to live in its desert home.

Roadrunners have short, rounded wings that are not good for flying. They usually run.

The Roadrunner

The roadrunner is a bird in the cuckoo family. Birds in this family have feet with two toes that face forward and two toes that face backward. Because of its toes, a roadrunner's tracks look like an "X."

Roadrunners are about the size of a skinny hen. They range from 18 to 24 inches (46 to 61 cm) long and weigh up to 24 ounces (680 g). Their tails are usually as long as their bodies. They have long, thin beaks and black feathers with white streaks. A bushy crest of feathers rises from the top of the bird's head. A crest is a row of feathers.

Where Do Roadrunners Live?

Roadrunners live in deserts throughout the southwestern United States. They can be found in the Mojave, Sonoran, Chihuahuan, and southern Great Basin deserts.

Most roadrunners live in flat areas where different kinds of desert scrub, such as sagebrush and chaparral, grow. Scrub is a growth of short plants and bushes. A roadrunner's coloring keeps it camouflaged among these desert plants. **Camouflage** is coloring or patterns that help an animal blend with its background.

How Have Roadrunners Adapted to Live in the Desert?

Roadrunners are specially built to live in deserts. A lot of the water their bodies need comes from the moist food they eat. To conserve more water, the bird's body reabsorbs water from its waste. This way, the roadrunner does not have to drink as much.

Roadrunners get rid of salt from their bodies differently than other birds do. Salt in a bird's

The camouflage coloring of this roadrunner
helps it blend in with its surroundings.

body builds up when it needs to sweat or as it
digests food. To digest is to break down food so
the body can use it. Most birds get rid of salt in
their liquid waste. However, roadrunners need
to conserve as much liquid as they can. They
use a special body part called a gland to rid the
body of salt. This gland is near the nose.

What a Roadrunner Eats

Roadrunners are omnivores. Omnivores eat both meat and plants. Most of a roadrunner's diet is meat, and it will eat almost anything it can catch. It eats plants only during cold, dry winters when it cannot find other food.

Common foods for the roadrunner are insects, lizards, mice, other birds, and snakes. Roadrunners are also one of the few animals that are fast enough to catch rattlesnakes. First, the roadrunner grabs the rattlesnake by its tail. Before the rattlesnake can bite the roadrunner, the bird swings the rattlesnake around and pounds its head on the ground until it dies.

Like other birds, roadrunners do not have teeth. They swallow their prey whole. Prey is an animal that is hunted as food. Roadrunners cannot eat all of a snake at one time. They carry it around, eating several inches at a time, until it is all gone. This can take several hours or longer.

To stay cool, roadrunners become less active during the hottest part of the day. Then they

▲ This roadrunner has caught a snake. Because roadrunners are fast, they are good hunters.

stop hunting and rest in the shade of desert scrub. When it becomes cooler, the birds become more active and begin hunting again.

This roadrunner is sitting on its eggs to keep them warm.

A Roadrunner's Life Cycle

Scientists think roadrunners mate for life. They find mates by making a series of cooing calls. Then the males put on a show for the females by dancing around.

The time roadrunners mate depends on where they live. Most roadrunners mate in the spring because it rains more then. It is easier to find prey to feed their chicks during the rainy season.

After mating, the male and female build a nest together. They find a small shrub or cactus and build a shallow nest out of twigs.

The female lays up to 12 eggs. After about 20 days, the eggs hatch. The parents take care of the chicks for about one month. During this time, baby roadrunners are in danger from predators. A predator is an animal that hunts and eats other animals as food. Coyotes, snakes, vultures, and hawks will eat young roadrunners.

The roadrunner has short, round wings, so it cannot fly well. To escape from predators, roadrunners usually walk or run along the ground. They can run up to 20 miles (32 km) per hour.

If the roadrunners survive childhood, they leave to find their own homes. When they are about 3 years old, they will find mates and begin to produce young. A roadrunner lives from seven to eight years.

You can see the stinger at the end of this giant desert hairy scorpion's tail.

The Giant Desert Hairy Scorpion

The giant desert hairy scorpion is the largest kind of scorpion in North America. It grows up to 5.5 inches (14 cm) long.

Scorpions are arachnids. All arachnids have four pairs of legs and a body with two parts. These parts are the cephalothorax and the abdomen. Giant desert hairy scorpions have a long body and a long, curling tail. A bulb-like poisonous stinger is at the end of the tail.

The giant desert hairy scorpion has light yellow legs. Its body color ranges from yellowish brown to dark brown. Yellow outlines each of its body segments. Dark brown hair covers most of its body. Scorpions use these hairs to sense smells and the movement of prey.

> This giant desert hairy scorpion is climbing down from its rocky home to hunt.

Where Do Giant Desert Hairy Scorpions Live?

Giant desert hairy scorpions live in deserts throughout the southwestern United States, as far east as Colorado. They mostly live in rocky areas of the desert. They hide among the cracks in the rock.

How Have Giant Desert Hairy Scorpions Adapted to Live in the Desert?

Giant desert hairy scorpions have adapted in many ways to live in deserts. Their bodies have a waxy coating. The coating stops moisture from leaving the body. Also, there is very little water in a scorpion's waste. These things help the scorpion conserve water in the dry desert.

Giant desert hairy scorpions do not need much energy. They spend most of their time resting. They digest their food very slowly so that energy is released a little at a time. Because of this, they do not need to eat often, sometimes only three or four times each year. This helps them survive during times when food is hard to find in the desert.

Giant desert hairy scorpions are cold-blooded. Cold-blooded animals have a body temperature that changes depending on the outside temperature. They will die if they become too cold or too hot. To adapt to the desert temperatures, giant desert hairy scorpions have become nocturnal. Nocturnal animals are active at night. It is cooler at night.

This giant desert hairy scorpion is about to
sting and eat a cricket.

What a Giant Desert Hairy Scorpion Eats

Giant desert hairy scorpions are **carnivores**.
Carnivores eat only meat. These large scorpions
eat mostly insects. They will also eat mice,
lizards, snakes, other scorpions, and small birds
if they can catch them. They have special

mouthparts called chelicerae that help them tear food. They grab prey with two lobster-like pedipalps that are used as feelers.

At night, giant desert hairy scorpions leave their burrows. They have excellent eyesight and can see special kinds of light. They use their eyesight and the hairs on their legs to catch prey. When prey comes near, it sends small vibrations along the ground. The hairs on the scorpion sense these vibrations. By the strength of the vibration, the scorpion can sense where the prey is and attack it.

The scorpion grabs the prey with its claw-like pedipalps. It then curls its tail over its head and stings its prey. The stinger works like a needle. It pricks the skin of its prey and injects venom, or poison, into the prey's body. The giant desert hairy scorpion keeps stinging its prey until the venom kills it.

The venom of the giant desert hairy scorpion is not strong enough to kill a healthy person. Its sting causes painful swelling, but no one has ever died from it.

The Life Cycle of the Giant Desert Hairy Scorpion

Scientists think that giant desert hairy scorpions use their sense of smell to find each other. Each scorpion releases special scents when it is ready to mate. Other scorpions can sense this scent.

Once a male has found a female, he and she grab each other's pedipalps. They dance around, back and forth and in circles, for several hours before mating.

The female gives birth to 25 to 35 live young. As they are born, she forms a birth basket by folding her legs. She catches the young in her legs and helps them climb to her back. Young scorpions ride around on their mother's back for about 15 days.

Scorpions do not have skeletons on the inside of their bodies as people do. Instead, they have a hard, outer exoskeleton. To grow, scorpions must shed the exoskeleton. They do this in a process called molting. To molt, the young scorpion grows inside its exoskeleton. The exoskeleton becomes harder and tighter as the young scorpion gets larger.

While this is happening, a soft, new exoskeleton grows underneath the old, hard exoskeleton. Finally, the old exoskeleton splits. The young scorpion crawls out of the old exoskeleton. It will molt again when its new exoskeleton becomes too small.

After its first molt, the young scorpion crawls down from its mother's back. It is on its own. Over time, it keeps molting. After about seven molts, giant desert hairy scorpions are fully grown. They live ten years or more. One giant desert hairy scorpion in a zoo lived to be 25 years old!

FUN FACT

Behind its fourth pair of legs, a scorpion has feathery sense organs called pectines. Pectines help the scorpion tell what kind of surface it is walking over. The scorpion is the only animal that has pectines.

Camels are the largest mammals that live in the desert biome.

The Camel

The camel is one of the few large mammals that live in deserts. A mammal is a warm-blooded animal with a backbone. Female mammals give birth to live young and feed them with milk from their bodies. Warm-blooded animals have a body temperature that usually stays the same, no matter what the temperature is outside.

Camels have a long, curved neck and tall, thin legs. They have a long face and a short tail. Most camels have tan fur, but they can be many colors, from white to black. They reach up to 7 feet (2 m) tall and weigh up to 1,600 pounds (725 kg).

There are two kinds of camels. All camels have humps. Bactrian camels have two humps, while dromedary camels have only one hump.

Where Do Camels Live?

Camels live in both hot and cold deserts. Dromedary camels live in deserts from northwestern India to southern Africa, including the Sahara Desert. Some of these camels also live in the deserts of Australia. All dromedary camels are domesticated. Domesticated means they are trained to be used by people. There are no wild dromedary camels.

Bactrian camels live in the cold deserts of Mongolia and China, including the Gobi Desert. There are still small herds of wild bactrian camels.

How Have Camels Adapted to Live in the Desert?

Both kinds of camels have adapted to live in deserts. Thick pads of rough skin cover camels' knees and feet. This helps them kneel and walk on the hot sand.

Camels have bushy eyebrows and two rows of long eyelashes. The extra eyelashes help protect the camels' eyes from blowing sand and dirt. The camel has a third eyelid that is thin and clear. The eyelid moves back and forth like a windshield wiper to help the camel clear sand

These dromedary camels live in the hot deserts of Africa.

from its eyes. During sandstorms, the camel protects its eyes with the clear eyelid, but can still see where it is going.

The camel also has large, slit-like nostrils that it can close when it wants. If sand begins blowing, the camel closes its nostrils. This keeps sand from entering its nose.

This camel is drinking water. It can go for up to two weeks without drinking again.

Water, Humps, and Hooves

Camels are expert at conserving water. Their waste is so dry that people can burn it as fuel. Throughout the day, camels can change their body temperature up to seven degrees. When it gets hot, they lower their body temperature.

This keeps them from sweating and losing moisture. Other mammals cannot do this. Camels can live with up to a 30-percent water loss. Other mammals will die if they lose about 15 percent of their water. When they find water, camels can drink one-third of their body weight at a time. Most other mammals would die from drinking so much water.

Camels store extra food in their humps as fat. A healthy camel's hump can weigh as much as 80 pounds (35 kg). When a camel needs food, it uses the fat in its hump. As the fat is used, the hump sags and may flop over on its side.

Bactrian camels are suited to life in the cold desert. They are smaller and heavier than dromedary camels. They also have longer, thicker hair to keep them warm in the cold. They shed some of their hair during the warm summer and grow it back again during winter. Their hooves are harder and stronger than dromedary hooves. This helps them climb over the small rocks in the cold desert. Dromedary hooves are wide and are better suited for walking over sand in the hot desert.

The camel's thick lips make it easy for it to eat thorny desert shrubs like this one.

What a Camel Eats

Camels are herbivores. Herbivores eat only plants. Camels spend up to 12 hours each day eating plants, such as grains, shrubs, and grass.

Camels have thick, tough lips. They use these lips to pull leaves and pieces from the rough, thorny plants that grow in deserts.

Camels regurgitate their food. To regurgitate is to bring the food back up out of the stomach into the mouth. After regurgitating, the camel chews its food more, usually 40 to 50 times before swallowing it again. By doing this, the camel can get energy from food that other animals have a hard time digesting.

The Life Cycle of the Camel

Camels are social animals. Social means they are friendly to each other and live together in groups. The size of the group depends on how much food is in an area.

When they are 3 to 6 years old, camels begin mating. Mating season is usually at the end of winter, right before the rainy season.

When males are ready to mate, they stick out a fleshy fold from their mouths and roar. They may try to scare other males away by raising their heads up and down. Sometimes males fight over females by biting each other's legs. The winner is the one that makes the other fall first.

About 15 months after mating, the female gives birth to one calf. She takes care of the calf for up to two years. Camels can live as long as 50 years.

You can see the raised bead-like scales of this Gila monster. The word "Gila" means warty skin.

The Gila Monster

Gila (HEE-lah) monsters are the largest lizard in North America. They can reach 22 inches (56 cm) and weigh up to 5 pounds (2 kg). They have long bodies and small heads with short, thick legs and tail. Each of their feet has five toes topped with strong claws.

Gila monsters are covered with raised, bead-like scales. A scale is a thick, tough piece of skin. The bumps are caused by small plates of bone in the skin called osteoderms.

Gila monsters are one of only two kinds of poisonous lizard in the world. They are colorful. Bright pink, yellow, or white patterns cover their brown or black bodies.

Where Do Gila Monsters Live?

Gila monsters live in the deserts of the southwestern United States and northern Mexico. They can be found in Utah, Nevada, California, Arizona, and New Mexico.

Gila monsters usually live alone in their **home range**. A home range is an area where an animal lives and looks for food. The Gila monster's home range is usually about 1 square mile (2.6 sq km). They have several burrows throughout their home ranges and spend up to 98 percent of their time in these burrows.

How Have Gila Monsters Adapted to Live in the Desert?

It is not always easy to find food in the desert. Gila monsters have a special adaptation to help them survive when food is hard to find. Their body turns extra food into fat and stores it in the tail. When the lizard cannot find food, it slowly turns the fat in its tail into energy that its body can use.

Like giant desert hairy scorpions, Gila monsters do not need much energy. Because they spend so much time resting, they rarely

This Gila monster is in its burrow. It may dig its own burrow or use other animals' burrows.

need to eat. If they can find large meals, the lizard may eat only two to three times each year.

Gila monsters are cold-blooded. When it gets too cold, the lizards **hibernate** in one of their burrows. To hibernate is to spend the winter in a sleep-like state. During these months, the lizards live off the fat stored in their tails.

What a Gila Monster Eats

Gila monsters are carnivores. They eat only
meat from animals, such as rabbits, birds, mice,
snakes, tortoises, and lizards. They often steal
eggs or newborns from other animals' nests to eat.

Gila monsters are the most active from March
through November. During the spring months,

many animals are giving birth to young. There are plenty of nests for Gila monsters to attack. During the cold winter months, they rest to conserve energy.

Gila monsters use their forked tongues to find prey. Their tongues pick up scents in the air. Every living thing releases a scent. Gila monsters use these scents to find the animals that released them. They keep flicking their tongues in the air and following the scent until they find their prey.

Sometimes Gila monsters swallow their prey whole. Other times, they bite and kill prey with their powerful jaws. Still other times, they use venom. To do this, they press their teeth into the prey's skin. Venom flows into special grooves in the Gila monster's teeth. Then it flows from the grooves into the prey's body. The Gila monster holds onto its prey until the venom has poisoned it.

Young Gila monsters can eat up to one-half their body weight. Adult Gila monsters can eat up to 35 percent of their body weight. Any food that is not used right away is stored as fat in the tail.

A Gila Monster's Life Cycle

Gila monsters' mating season is between April and June. When they are ready to mate, the male and female release special scents. The male lizard uses his tongue to sense the female's scent. He then will follow the scent until he finds her.

After mating, the female lays from 2 to 15 oval eggs. Larger females usually lay more eggs. A female uses her claws to dig a hole in sand or soil about 5 inches (13 cm) deep. Then she lays the eggs in the hole and buries them. After this, the female leaves the eggs.

The eggs need heat to develop. The sun warms the sand or soil, and this heats the eggs. The eggs develop over the next several months. The eggs hatch the next April through June.

The colorful newly hatched Gila monsters are about 4 inches (10 cm) long. They are on their own as soon as they hatch.

Predators, such as hawks, coyotes, and owls, try to eat Gila monsters. If predators come near, the lizards will run into a nearby burrow. If they are not close to one, they hiss and puff up their

This Gila monster is using its tongue to find the scent of its mate.

bodies to look larger. To fight them off, the lizards bite their attacker. They try to get venom into their enemies' bodies. Gila monsters usually use their venom only to attack predators. If predators do not eat them, Gila monsters can live up to 20 years.

As people move into the deserts, animals like this giant desert hairy scorpion have less space to live.

What Will Happen to Desert Animals?

The desert provides a special habitat for the animals that live there. A habitat is a place where an animal or plant usually lives. Many plants and animals that live in deserts could not survive in other biomes.

Over time, people have begun to change the deserts. Large scrub areas of the desert have been cleared to make farms or to build cities. When this happens, desert animals lose their homes. Food may become harder to find. Some animals may become **endangered**. Endangered means a kind of animal may die out in the wild.

> People need to save the Gila monster's habitat, or the lizard will continue to be endangered.

How Are Desert Animals Doing?

The Gila monster is one desert animal that is endangered. Scientists do not know how many are alive because they are hard to find and study. People have cleared mesquite from areas of the Gila monster's habitat. This leaves fewer areas in which the animal can live. Many people also catch wild Gila monsters and try to sell them as pets. This is against the law in both the United States and Mexico where the lizards live. Other people are afraid of the Gila monster, so they kill it. They think that its poison might kill them if they are bitten, even though the poison is not deadly for healthy people.

Bactrian camels are also endangered. Scientists think there are only 1,000 of these camels left in the wild. The main danger they face is habitat loss. People are building cities in the Gobi Desert. This makes it hard for the camels to find food and water. In China, some people hunt the camels for meat.

Unless people work to save the deserts, other desert animals, such as the giant desert hairy scorpion and the roadrunner, may become endangered, too. Some people are saving desert animals by creating national parks and deserts. It is against the law to build or hunt in these places. If we save the deserts, the animals that live there will survive in their homes for a long time.

Quick Facts

Giant desert hairy scorpions raise their tails high in the air when they are about to sting their prey.

Giant desert hairy scorpions are drawn to moisture. They usually stay away from people, but will enter newly built homes to be near the moisture found in drying cement.

Male gila monsters sometimes fight each other. Their fighting is like wrestling. The winning lizard pins the other lizard to the ground. This fighting usually does not hurt males. The losing lizard leaves the area.

The roadrunner is New Mexico's state bird.

The roadrunner is so fast that it can leap up and grab a hummingbird in its beak.

Early settlers named the roadrunner after seeing it run in the tracks made by their wagon wheels.

A camel's skull has a thick bony ridge above each eye. These ridges stick out from the head. They act as natural shades by blocking the overhead sun. This way, the sun stays out of the camel's eyes.

Glossary

biome (BYE-ohm)—large regions, or areas, in the world that have similar climates, soil, plants, and animals

burrows (BUR-ohz)—holes or tunnels in the ground where animals live

camouflage (KAM-o-flaj)—colors, shapes, and patterns that make something blend in with its background

carnivores (KAHR-nuh-vorz)—animals that eat only meat

conserve (kuhn-SURV)—to save or protect something

digests (dye-JESTS)—breaks down food so the body can use it

endangered (en-DAYN-jurd)—a plant or animal species that is in danger of dying out

hibernate (HEYE-bur-nayt)—to spend the winter in a sleep-like state

home range (HOME RAYNJ)—an area where an animal has found all the things it needs to live

Internet Sites and Addresses

Biomes of the World
http://mbgnet.mobot.org
Learn information about the different biomes around the world and where they are located.

National Park Service
http://www.nps.gov
Discover the special features of different national parks and where each park is located.

Chihuahuan Desert Research Institute
P.O. Box 1332
Alpine, TX 79831

The Living Desert
47-900 Portola Avenue
Palm Desert, CA 92260

Maturango Museum, Museum of Upper Mojave Desert
100 East Las Flores Avenue
Ridgecrest, CA 93555

Sonoran Desert State Park
P.O. Box 40427
Tucson, AZ 85717

Books to Read

Lalley, Patrick and Lalley, Janet. *Desert Scientists.* Austin, TX: Steck-Vaughn, 2001.

Steele, Christy. *Deserts.* Austin, TX: Steck-Vaughn, 2000.

Index

DATE DUE			

591.754
STE

32878010040252
Steele, Christy.

Desert animals